HOW TO TURN

WISDOM CURRENCY

TO MONEY

MONEY MAGNET SERIES

Applying the principles of the Kingdom to make wealth.

IREDAFENEVESHO OWOLABI

1

KEYS FOR BIBLE TRANSLATIONS USED:

AMP - The Amplified Bible, **GNB** - Good News Bible, **MSG** - The Message Translation, **NASB** – New American Standard Bible, **NCV** – New Century Version, **NIV** - New International Version, **NKJV** - New King James Version, **NLT** - New Living Translation, **TLB** - The Living Bible.

The revelations herein are expressed from the author's perspective and spiritual insight on the subject matter covered. It is published with the understanding that the writer is not rendering legal, medical, financial or other professional service. If legal advice or other expert assistance is required, the services of a competent professional should be sought. The author and publisher are in no way liable for any misuse of the material.

DEDICATION

To the King of kings who has inspired me to put this masterpiece together.

TABLE OF CONTENTS

CHAPTER ONE

WISDOM AND MONEY: THE CONNECTION

Wisdom has many sides to its definition and they are very relevant for making wealth here on earth and for complete fulfilment in life. Paul described wisdom as having many-sides in its various applications (Eph 3:10 AMP). Among these many-sided aspects of wisdom is the concept of wisdom as a kingdom currency. Intensive research and study of scripture has shown that wisdom is a currency of heaven that can be used to exchange for things which earthly money cannot buy like long life, honor, peace and other precious commodities. In addition to that, it can also be converted into any earthly currency and can provide even the things earthly money can buy. As a result, wisdom is a more superior currency to pound sterling, dollar, euro, naira, etc

What does it mean to Be Wise?

According to Vine's Dictionary of New Testament Words, there are two very important Greek words translated as wisdom in the New Testament and they are **_"Sophia"_** *"phronesis"*. Sophia means insight into the true nature of things, or insight into reality. Phronesis on the other hand, refers to the ability to act on insights and convert them into reality. In order words, phronesis is the application of Sophia. Phronesis is practical wisdom while Sophia is theoretical wisdom. While Sophia is insight into reality, phronesis is the ability to convert the insights into reality. Both definitions of wisdom as stated above are highly relevant for understanding the concept of wisdom. For example, Sophia is what gives a man the idea the write a book or start a globally relevant business. Through Sophia, the intending writer or potential business man has an insight into what the book or business will be about and a picture of what it should look like. But phronesis gives him the ability, to act in the direction of converting that idea into reality, by causing him to apply the insight in an organized manner to produce the actions that would bring about the reality that was once just an idea. There are several other examples of how sophia and phronesis operate. Some people operate with sophia but lack phronesis, hence they have many ideas, insights and visions and have never been able to bring any into fruition, neither are they in the process. *I pray for you today, that all your ideas begin to receive divine energy and practical wisdom that will turn them into reality in Jesus name!*

I would like to state here that no book is exhaustive enough when it comes to dealing with the nature and the definitions of wisdom. No teacher is deep enough to fully express the depths of the wisdom of God. One of the foremost teachers of all time, who is reputed for his depth of revelations at a time, tried to dig into the wells of spiritual discovery in a bid to completely unravel and search out the wisdom of God. During his spiritual search, he dug and kept digging but could not get to the end of his search. This continued until he yelled out saying *"Oh, the depth of the riches of the wisdom and knowledge of God! How unsearchable his judgments, and his paths beyond tracing out! (Rom 11:33 NIV)"* By this exclamation, Paul the Apostle disclosed some powerful qualities of the wisdom of God. One quality of wisdom disclosed here is that **the depth of wisdom is so much that it is impossible to completely search it all out at once**. Most of the valuable metals and precious stones on earth today like gold, silver and diamond are by nature hid under great depths of earth or underneath rocks. These treasures need to be dug out, and mined for several years before all the precious deposits are completely searched out by excavation. Sometimes, the rocks would need to be forcefully blown up with dynamites in order to locate the treasures. At this writing, eight out of the ten deepest gold mines in the world are located in South Africa. Among these eight is the

TauTona gold mine. Mining operations began in TauTona around 1962 with the construction of 800km of tunnels. As the mining operation progressed, TauTona's mine life was estimated to end in 2015 [4]. This gives us an idea of the long period of time normally spent and the large amount of resources invested in order to dig out all the gold deposits in a mine. Despite the depth of the gold mines of South Africa, miners have been able to dig out all the deposits in some mines in the space of years and have also been able to estimate the mine life of several mines through the help of technology. But this cannot be said of the wisdom mine because its depths are unsearchable and its paths, past finding out. No sage has been able to estimate the mine life of the wisdom deposits in our kingdom. Neither has anyone been able to successfully get to the depths of the wisdom currency because of its superabundance. This is what led Paul, the Apostle to refer to the riches of wisdom as unsearchable. If this is so, then it is safe to say that there is no finite definition of wisdom. This is so because the wisdom of God is innumerable in all its aspects. The definitions of different sages who have shared their perspectives on wisdom based on scriptures are very correct. However, wisdom in all its aspects have not yet been fully discovered because wisdom is infinite, hence new perspectives and definitions will be given to the church at different times in history by the Spirit of God. Paul made this point clearer when he wrote to Ephesus. Let us consider his statement below:

[The purpose is] that THROUGH THE CHURCH THE COMPLICATED, MANY-SIDED WISDOM OF GOD IN ALL ITS INFINITE VARIETY AND INNUMERABLE ASPECTS might now be made known to the angelic rulers and authorities (principalities and powers) in the heavenly sphere.

Eph 3:10 AMP

Having established this foundation, I will proceed to define one of the innumerable aspects of the wisdom of God. *Wisdom can be seen as a heavenly currency which grants its possessor insight into reality, provides him solutions to problems including those which earthly currencies cannot resolve and gives ability to discern and apply the right approach to any situation.* Wisdom is a currency that has been reserved exclusively for the citizens of the kingdom to display as they bring glory to the King of kings and the Lord of lords. The wisdom currency which those who lived before Christ tapped into is nothing to be compared to that which has been made available unto us who are in Christ, and as such, are kingdom citizens.

We do, however, speak a message of wisdom among the mature, but not the wisdom of this age or of the rulers of this age, who are coming to nothing. No, WE SPEAK OF GOD'S SECRET WISDOM, A WISDOM THAT HAS BEEN HIDDEN AND THAT GOD DESTINED FOR OUR GLORY BEFORE TIME BEGAN.

1 Cor 2:6-8 NIV

Wisdom has been appointed unto those who will become citizens of the Kingdom in the post resurrection era (after the resurrection of Christ). It was ordained for those who are in Christ Jesus to explore in a greater dimension than that which the kings, priests and prophets of old could access. It would be foolhardy not to enjoy this currency which has been preserved exclusively for kingdom citizens if you are born again.

Wisdom is a Kingdom Currency that can be converted to Money

In order to answer this question properly, we need to remind ourselves of the definition of the word currency. Currency, simply put, is any commodity that is used and accepted in a particular country and at a particular time, as money for exchange of goods and services[3]. Just as every nation on earth has its own currency or a currency peculiar to it, which its citizens and residents transact with, the heavenly country known as the kingdom of heaven has a currency. It is therefore pleasing to announce to you, my beloved reader, that wisdom is a kingdom currency. The scripture below buttresses this line of thought.

TO BE WISE IS AS GOOD AS BEING RICH; in fact, it is better. YOU CAN GET ANYTHING BY EITHER WISDOM OR MONEY, but being wise has many advantages.

Eccl 7:11-12 TLB

Wow... What an amazing truth is revealed by Solomon, the sage king in the verse above. He says "...to be wise is as good as being rich..." Why? This is because wisdom in itself is a kingdom currency in the kingdom of heaven, among other commodities in the kingdom currency system just like gold, silver, dollars, pounds, etc, is in earthly kingdoms. Solomon also stated that wisdom is even better than earthly riches, and if we study the other books written by him on the subject, we can tell why. In one of his writings, he said:

She (wisdom) is more precious than jewels; and nothing you desire compares with her (wisdom). Long life is in her (wisdom's) right hand; IN HER (wisdom's) LEFT HAND ARE RICHES and honor. Her (wisdom's) ways are pleasant ways, and all her paths are peace.

Proverbs 3:15-17 NASB

(Emphasis added)

I also love the way The Living Bible translates the above verse. It says, *"For such wisdom is far more valuable than precious jewels. Nothing else compares with it. WISDOM GIVES: a long, good life, RICHES, honor, pleasure, peace." (Proverbs 3:15-17 TLB).* Remember this scripture above is been used as a reference to explain how wisdom is a kingdom currency. That is why the word "riches", is made to stand out, not because riches is the most important thing in that verse. Wisdom, when accessed, harnessed, and converted, produces riches. The wisest king in the Old Testament, was recorded to be the richest king of all time before the King of kings, Jesus came on the scene. This was a function of the wisdom the man possessed and was able to harness and convert. Solomon's riches did not just come by magic, wisdom produced them.

Oh, the depth of the RICHES OF THE WISDOM and knowledge of God! How unsearchable his judgments, and his paths beyond tracing out!

Rom 11:33 NIV

The word riches in the above verse, is from the Greek word which literally means money and possessions and figuratively means abundance. Remember that money and currency are two interchangeable words which are synonymous to each other. It is therefore easy to see that wisdom is a currency by virtue of the statement in that verse. The term "riches of wisdom" can also be interpreted as "abundance of wisdom", *"currency of wisdom"*, "wealth of wisdom" or "possessions of wisdom". This further gives an indication that wisdom is a currency.

CHAPTER TWO

THE VALUE OF WISDOM CURRENCY

Many young ladies today do not know the value of wisdom in a man. They would rather get involved with a man who can afford to buy them luxuries whether or not he has a future. They really do not care the way he makes the money being lavished on them, as long as they get to have their expenses covered sufficiently by the man's questionable wealth. Even when responsible suitors come their way, they push them aside on the grounds of wealth not regarding his potential, and his wisdom currency. When I and my precious jewel got wedded, it was a time in Nigeria when there was economic recession in the land. I had just published my first book, I did not have the millions in my earthly bank account then, but I knew I had all I needed to take care of a wife and to raise a home. This knowledge was an insight sponsored by the wisdom currency. From what I gathered from my wife, among the different wonderful things she saw and admired in me was the great wisdom bestowed on me and how that I was already applying this wisdom. She said she did not look out for my earthly riches to make her decision because she wanted something that was more valuable than riches in her man. She knew that wisdom was far better than riches, because in the process of time riches will pursue after a wise man. This lady understood the value of the wisdom currency, and by the grace of God, we have enjoyed divine provisions from the day we walked down the aisle. This heavenly currency has been sustaining us in a superabundant measure, and the story only gets better. It pays to know the value of wisdom currency because that way, you would not be carried away by crave for material wealth at the expense of wisdom currency. The scripture below puts everything in the right perspective:

Blessed is the man who finds wisdom, the man who gains understanding, for she is more profitable than silver and YIELDS BETTER RETURNS THAN GOLD. She (wisdom) is MORE PRECIOUS THAN RUBIES; NOTHING YOU DESIRE CAN COMPARE WITH HER. LONG LIFE is in her (wisdom's) right hand; in her (wisdom's) left hand are RICHES AND HONOR.

Proverbs 3:13-16
NIV (emphasis added)

In Proverbs 3:15, the Bible says that all the things to be desired in this world cannot be compared to the wisdom currency. This is because wisdom as a currency of heaven has a comparative advantage over any other currency of value in any earthly nation today. It is amazing how most people, including some kingdom citizens, only measure wealth in terms of earthly currency and hence value material things over wisdom currency. They seem to take for granted the invaluable worth of this heavenly currency because they are ignorant of this truth; hence they are bankrupt of this heavenly commodity. I love the way the Bible estimates the value of wisdom currency, in comparison to other renowned currencies of this world. It says:

Happy is the man that findeth wisdom, and the man that getteth understanding. FOR THE MERCHANDISE OF IT IS BETTER THAN THE MERCHANDISE OF SILVER, AND THE GAIN THEREOF THAN FINE GOLD. SHE IS MORE PRECIOUS THAN RUBIES: AND ALL THE THINGS THOU CANST DESIRE ARE NOT TO BE COMPARED UNTO HER.

Proverbs 3:13-15

From the above verse we can see how wisdom is a more potent currency than silver, gold or rubies. If you study carefully, you would observe that Solomon the writer was trying to communicate to us, the comparative value added advantage of wisdom currency. No doubts, wisdom has more value than the most valuable currencies of any nation on earth.

In the days of old, gold was recognized as a currency for transaction and as a medium of exchange. As a matter of fact, gold was used to support the currencies that were considered legal tender in their nation of origin as far back as 1453. Gold was used as money because it was such an excellent measure of value. Even during wars and upheavals, and in times of crisis, gold is known to always retain its value. Although, gold only holds industrial value now, it remains the oldest currency in the world and is still respected even when national paper monies lose value. That is why most nations often bank gold in private reserves, because till date, it is one of the best known items that can store value in earthly systems[5]. It was also used as the world reserve currency up until 1971 when President Nixon discontinued its use as the standard measure. Until the use of gold standard was stopped, no country could simply print their paper currencies except they possessed an equal amount of gold in their reserve[6]. Despite the role which gold has played in earthly nations, wisdom and all the other kingdom currencies are significantly of greater value any day and any time. *Anyone who possesses the wisdom currency is wealthier than the richest man in the systems of this world.* It is only matter of when such a person discovers the value of the kingdom currency and learns to withdraw and convert it into tangible equivalents.

If gold and silver are known as highly esteemed commodities even to this day, and Solomon, in the above verse tells us wisdom is more profitable and of higher value compared to them, it means the wisdom currency is deserving of our attention. As you can see that even though gold and silver have played great roles in the world economy from ancient times till this day, the kingdom currency of wisdom is of greater value. *This means that anyone who possesses wisdom, no matter the economic uncertainty of the earthly nation he resides can buy anything, at anytime.* The extent, to which anyone will enjoy this kingdom currency of wisdom, depends on how much he values wisdom, knows its exchange rates, and knows how to convert it to earthly equivalents. We must therefore be more conscious of this wisdom currency to a greater level than the level to which citizens of earthly nations are of earthly currencies. This will cause us to truly enjoy kingdom currency in such a way that we can convert it to material wealth, honor, riches, plus a fulfilling, healthy, peaceful and robust long life. *I declare divine ability upon you to begin to merchandise and transact profitably in the kingdom currency of wisdom in Jesus name! I banish lack from your life, and from your generations yet unborn by this revelation in Jesus name!*

The Wisdom Currency as an Investment Capital

In the mathematical world, there is a concept known as **Simple Interest.** When we invest a sum of money in a savings account over a period of **time (t)**, the account earns us **interest (I)**, depending on the bank's **rate (r)** and on the **time duration (t)** in which that money was invested. The initial amount invested is known as the **principal (P)**. Therefore the formula for simple interest is said to be *I=Prt*. This concept is used when someone wants to get a capital loan to start a business from a bank. For every loan, an interest is compounded on the actual amount borrowed. This interest is compounded over a proposed time duration in which the loan will be paid back. The loan which was given as capital to start a business is known as the principal.

WISDOM IS THE PRINCIPAL thing; therefore get wisdom...

Prov 4:7

The verse above, in a very concise manner, expresses to us that if we possess the kingdom currency of wisdom, we can establish any enterprise. This is because "wisdom is the principal thing...", therefore anyone who possesses the kingdom currency of wisdom and knows how to convert it to earthly equivalents has the principal or capital he needs to start any business or build any enterprise. This goes to show how things operate in earthly kingdoms where you hear people say they lack capital or the principal amount needed for their businesses to take off. *But in the kingdom of heaven, no kingdom citizen lacks capital because wisdom is the capital; it is the principal you need to bring about anything you desire or to start any enterprise.* If the capital you require is money, a plot of land, a shop, a vehicle, an equipment or expertise, the wisdom currency is capable of bringing each and any of these into your hands in a way that is peculiar and unique. The problem faced by many young and aspiring entrepreneurs today is that they allow the thought of lack of capital to drown the passion they once nursed for a great idea. They focus on their lack of material resources or things money can buy, and they lose grip of the immaterial resource they possess. They fail to understand that immaterial resources can always be converted to any material resource you can think of if properly accessed and converted. This makes it so difficult for a lot of people to enjoy kingdom currency and what it avails. The lack of any capital is a reflection of a lack of the wisdom required to kick-start, jump-start or run that business. If you are in such a dire situation, and you also want to find a solution to it, know that what you have in your hand is a solution bank tailored to meet such needs. Let's examine an antidote below:

BUT IF ANY OF YOU LACKS WISDOM, LET HIM ASK OF GOD, who gives to all men generously and without reproach, and it will be given to him.

James 1:5 NASB

Superabundant provision has been made for every kingdom citizen not to lack this wisdom currency. This provision is stored up in heaven's treasury and if you must ask God the King for this wisdom currency, then you must know Him for yourself and have a working relationship with him. Scripture tells us that we have a generous King who is also a Father to us. If He gives to all men generously without reproach, how much more will he give this currency to His own children? He said you can ask for more if your kingdom currency of wisdom is deficient or lacking in supply. It means that no kingdom citizen has an excuse for not accessing the wisdom currency. Many kingdom citizens are not enjoying this kingdom currency because they ask for the wrong things all the time. Hence they remain stagnant in life and do not experience true progress. For example, most average young graduates immediately after their tertiary education, begin to seek for ways to acquire money, they apply for a job, or pursue some other things. When it seems like all their efforts have yielded no result, they resort to going back into school for another degree or a higher degree. The challenge however, is that most times people often take these steps with little or no plans to gain more wisdom for the next phase of their lives. While all these things are good in themselves, they are no guarantee of having fulfillment and satisfaction in life except they are done with the guidance of the Spirit of wisdom.

CHAPTER THREE

THE LOCATION OF WISDOM CURRENCY

Most governments on earth have a vault where treasures like gold, silver, precious stones, highly classified documents, etc, are stored. These vaults are highly protected and under maximum security surveillance. It could be a repository, a treasury, a bank reserve, or a store house depending on what works for that country or kingdom. An estimate of about 25% of the entire world's gold is said to be housed in the Federal Reserve Bank which is located in Manhattan, New York. Large portions of the gold in this vault were deposited during and after World War II because many nations wanted their gold reserves in a safe place. At this writing, the vault has remained the largest known store of monetary gold in the world. The vault had an estimate of 508,000 gold bars, which weighed about 6,350 tons as at 2015. This Federal Reserve stores gold deposits in its vault on behalf of account holders, like the United States government, governments of other foreign nations, central banks, and international organizations[6]. Similarly, *the Kingdom of God has a very safe and secure spiritual location where all its treasures are stored. This location is named after*

the man who is known as the first begotten from the dead. This reserve is called Christ because it is named after Jesus Christ the Son of the living God. **This spiritual location can be seen as Kingdom Reserve.**

My purpose is that they may be encouraged in heart and united in love, so that they may have the full riches of complete understanding, in order that they may know THE MYSTERY OF GOD, NAMELY, CHRIST, IN WHOM ARE HIDDEN ALL THE TREASURES OF WISDOM and knowledge.

Col 2:2-3 NIV

According to Henry Thayer's lexicon, the Greek word for "treasures" in the above verse is "thesauros". It actually refers to the place in which good and precious things are collected and laid up. That is a coffer, treasury, storehouse or repository. The word also refers to the actual deposits and wealth which are laid up and stored inside the treasury. By this simple exposition, it is easy to understand what the scripture above is trying to communicate to us. In order to locate and access this reserve, you need to get to the word of God because, Jesus Christ, the one after whom the Kingdom reserve is named is also known as "the word of God".

Then I saw heaven opened, and a white horse was standing there. Its rider was named Faithful and True, for he judges fairly and wages a righteous war. His eyes were like flames of fire, and on his head were many crowns. A NAME WAS WRITTEN ON HIM that no one understood except himself. He wore a robe dipped in blood, AND HIS TITLE WAS THE WORD OF GOD.

Rev 19:11-13 NLT

You may wonder how possible it is to say Christ is the place where these treasures are located. This is what Paul refers to as the mystery of God in Colossians 2:2-3. The word mystery in this verse means a secret or a hidden thing. The Bible however, gives several references where we are made to understand that God has a place of refuge, which is sometimes referred to as a secret place, and at other times, a hiding place, dwelling place, refuge or fortress. A few scriptures are given below to validate this revelation.

LORD, THOU HAST BEEN OUR DWELLING PLACE in all generations.

Ps 90:1

Here, Moses makes a very mysterious statement by referring to the Lord as a dwelling place. That statement may startle the uninformed a bit but in the very next chapter, another boggling truth is revealed emphasizing   the same truth.

HE THAT DWELLETH IN THE SECRET PLACE OF THE MOST HIGH shall abide under the shadow of the Almighty. I WILL SAY OF THE LORD, HE IS MY REFUGE AND MY FORTRESS: my God; in him will I trust.

Psalms 91:1-2

The most High God, the creator who was not created has a secret place. It was not revealed to the men of old until Christ came to the earth. The secret place of the most high is called Christ. The Psalmist calls the Lord his refuge and fortress. A refuge is known as a place that provides safety, security and shelter. On the other hand, a fortress is known as a large strong building or group of buildings, which provides fortification and military defense against attack. Again, the psalmist does not only refer to a secret place of the most high, but he calls the Lord a place, a refuge, a fortress. This is mind boggling! But that is not all; there are more insights to strengthen this revelation, just read on.

THOU ART MY HIDING PLACE and my shield: I HOPE IN THY WORD.

Ps 119:114-115

The word "hiding place" was derived from the same Hebrew word from which "secret place" was translated. It is from the Hebrew word, "sether" and it means a covering, hiding place of protection or a secret place. Again, the Psalmist refers to the Lord as a place. This time he is more specific and says, "I hope in thy word". And Jesus Christ is the word of God. The psalmist only had a vague insight into this place because Christ had not been revealed in his days. Due to the deep fellowship he had with God he got the opportunity to have a glimpse of this place called Christ on a superficial level. Isaiah, the prophet, went further into this secret which was concealed from the men of old, but revealed to us in the new covenant. Here is what he said:

AND I WILL GIVE THEE THE TREASURES of darkness, AND HIDDEN RICHES OF SECRET PLACES, that thou mayest know that I, the Lord, which call thee by thy name, am the God of Israel.

Isa 45:3

The word secret place is used again and this refers to a place where money, hard currency, valuables, treasures and riches are also hidden. This place is called Christ and Paul tells us that all the treasures of wisdom are hid in Christ, the secret place of the most high. All of the treasures of the kingdom of heaven are accessible through the word of God and Christ is the word of God. The simple truth is that, to access any kingdom currency, you need to go to the word of God. This is one way to locate the wisdom currency and all other commodities in the kingdom reserve. *The word of God is God's wisdom bank given so we can access freely, convert abundantly and use generously the wisdom currency contained therein*. No kingdom citizen can stay ignorant of God's word and still make the most of, or enjoy any kingdom currency. The Holy Spirit can be seen as the Governor of the Kingdom reserve.

But just as it is written, "Things which eye has not seen and ear has not heard, And which have not entered the heart of man, all that God has prepared for those who love Him". For to us God revealed them through the Spirit; for the Spirit searches all things, even the depths of God. Now we have received, not the spirit of the world, but the Spirit who is from God, that we might know the things freely given to us by God,

1 Cor 2:9-10, 12 NASB

The angels of God can be seen as the resource personnel and managers in the kingdom reserve, appointed to serve those who are to become heirs of salvation or heirs of the Kingdom. I love the way The Living Bible puts it. It brings to mind the idea of a bank staff assigned to assist you in everything that pertains to your account, like an account officer or a customer care staff in the bank. They help and care for kingdom citizens in maintaining, and running their accounts and deliver to them their withdrawals whenever the account holder wants to access his bounties.

...for THE ANGELS ARE ONLY SPIRIT-MESSENGERS SENT OUT TO HELP AND CARE for those who are to receive His salvation.

Heb 1:14 TLB

You can withdraw from the Kingdom reserve (the word), ask the Governor (Holy Spirit) and demand that your service personnel (angels) in the kingdom reserve lead you to the vault of kingdom currency where you can make withdrawals. When you do, you would be amazed how much of the wisdom currency you would enjoy. Daniel knew this secret when there was a big situation in Babylon. The king had seen a terrible dream that gave him sleepless nights. He wanted to know the interpretation of the dream but could not remember the dream. He then asked his magicians, sorcerers and astrologers to tell him the dream and interpret. The so called wise men could not tell him his dream because it seemed impossible for anyone to know the dream of another man even if they sleep side by side on the same bed. The so called wise men did not have the wisdom currency, but they called themselves wise men because they had the counterfeit version of the authentic wisdom currency. They made a remarkable statement that further buttresses the location of the kingdom currency.

And it is a rare thing that the king requireth, AND THERE IS NONE OTHER THAT CAN SHEW IT BEFORE THE KING, EXCEPT THE GODS, WHOSE DWELLING IS NOT WITH FLESH.

Dan 2:11-12

When Daniel heard that the king ordered the execution of all the wise men including him, he made enquiries and discovered that the thing the king wanted was accessible to him and his friends. He therefore showed up and requested for time to access the vault of kingdom currency. He and his friends sought God and received the answer in a night vision. Remember our definition of wisdom – the insight into the true nature of things. God gave Daniel the insight into what the king truly dreamt about by wisdom.

Then Daniel went in, and desired of the king that he would give him time, and that he would shew the king the interpretation. Then Daniel went to his house, and made the thing known to Hananiah, Mishael, and Azariah, his companions: That they would desire mercies of the God of heaven concerning this secret; that Daniel and his fellows should not perish with the rest of the wise men of Babylon. Then was the secret revealed unto Daniel in a night vision. Then Daniel blessed the God of heaven. Daniel answered and said, Blessed be the name of God forever and ever: for wisdom and might are his:

Dan 2:16-20

Is Wisdom Currency another Get-Rich-Quick Scheme?

Pride leads to conflict; THOSE WHO TAKE ADVICE ARE WISE. WEALTH FROM GET-RICH-QUICK SCHEMES QUICKLY DISAPPEARS; wealth from hard work grows over time.

Proverbs 13:10-11 NLT

If you read verse 10 of the verses above from the God's Word Translation, it says "...those who take advice gain wisdom..." this is another way to access the kingdom currency of wisdom. By taking heed to advice and counsels like the ones in verse 11 above. Don't get into "get-rich-quick" schemes, ponzi schemes and the different forms of gamble, prevalent in this greedy and lust driven society because, you are different from the ordinary mankind by new birth. Leave those schemes for the "unkingdomised" folks. Some say their purpose for getting into get-rich-quick schemes and ponzi schemes is to raise enough capital to start a business. But that is one of the most self deceptive statements anyone can tell himself as a kingdom citizen because wisdom is your capital. No ponzi scheme can ever give you seed money because they were not designed that way. They were designed to give bread money that will keep its victims spending on luxuries and liabilities, and this keeps them coming back to ask for more. They trap their victims with wonderful promises of grandeur to those who bring more people to them. Ponzi schemes are designed to make its organizers extremely wealthy through greed, crave for instant wealth and unearned gratification by its victims. As long as such victims keep receiving handouts, the ponzi scheme remains in business. And though these handouts may appear big in the eyes of their prey, they are truly monies of other gullible individuals who are also victims. The system is wired to give a highly temporal gratification to its victims thereby hypnotizing its victims and enslaving them.

A ponzi scheme is a flawed financial system, in which old investors receive payment through returns which are brought in by new investors. Such scheme blossoms only when it gets new investors; and the absence of such marks its end, leaving the most recent donors with great losses[8]. There was a particular ponzi scheme that wreaked havoc on so many Nigerians. It is known as the Mavrodi Mundial Moneybox (MMM) and is said to have been founded by a Russian, Sergei Mavrodi, his brother Vyacheslav Mavrodi, and a woman Olga Melnikova[9]. Over three million Nigerians fell for this scheme despite obvious warnings against such schemes. MMM became popular in Nigeria in July 2016 and in December 2016, the organizers suspended payments to the shock of its victims. In March 2017, the Nigeria Deposit

Insurance Commission (NDIC) stated that Nigerians lost about 18 billion naira to MMM in 2016. According to the Daily Trust, about 109 ponzi schemes were still trending in Nigeria despite the crash of MMM as at April 16, 2017 as many MMM recruits went to other ponzi schemes to take refuge. After the Federal Government of Nigeria officially announced economic recession in September 2016, this particular scheme became popular in Nigeria[8]. Apparently, Nigeria was a good market place for MMM as many of its citizens, under the shockwave of recession began to make frantic efforts to survive. Hence many entered into this scheme as an alternative means of survival.

As nice and sincere as that excuse sounds, it does not validate the action taken. Anyone who keeps making excuses and blaming others for the poor state of his personal life is not ready to enjoy the kingdom currency. The government of your earthly nation may not be doing enough to help you, but that is still not an excuse for failure. This is because there are people under that same government, and in the same situation as yours, who are making a difference in their lives by doing the right things and taking wisdom oriented steps. The fact that there is famine in the land does not therefore mean anyone should do anything just to get money, especially as a kingdom citizen. The saddening reality is that, so many kingdom citizens in Nigeria, who ought to know better fell prey to this sham called MMM. Some pastors from different churches contacted me and tried to persuade me to get involved in it but I declined because I knew from scripture that no ponzi scheme would ever be sustained. Even though it may look like it is paying off at a given moment, it is only a matter of when it will fail, and not a matter of if it will fail. And when it does fail it leads its victims to poverty, depression and even suicide as was the case in Russia[8].

GREEDY PEOPLE TRY TO GET RICH QUICK BUT DON'T REALIZE THEY'RE HEADED FOR POVERTY.

Prov 28:22 NLT

As kingdom citizens, we must know that we are not money chasers; we are to be chased by prosperity and those of us who know who we are, are never victims of such schemes. If Jesus the King tarries, many more schemes will surface and there would always be victims of such schemes as long as people remain greedy and too lazy to think. But if you are reading this book, you don't have to be a victim of such. Anyone who craves quick wealth will become a prey of lust and will not know when he begins to violate kingdom principles of wealth. Such persons will never harness their true potential and ability and may never be able to enjoy kingdom currency. God wants us to learn how to grow over time in wealth while fulfilling purpose and doing what we were born to do, hence He gave us the wisdom currency to help us achieve this.

CHAPTER FOUR

THE BENEFITS OF

WISDOM CURRENCY

1. *Wisdom currency distinguishes its possessor even among other trained and skilled experts.*

The wisdom currency gave Daniel and his friends a great edge over their contemporaries. The wisdom currency can give you outstanding insight beyond what people who were reputed for skill and knowledge can have. For example, as a student, you can be so endowed with the wisdom currency that even the veterans and professors in that field would marvel at the degree of your intellectual prowess. Every student needs the wisdom currency to be exceptional in their academics. Even masons, artisans, fashion designers, engineers, doctors, lawyers, and so on, need this currency. That is what will distinguish you among others and give a competitive advantage in whatever business you do. Money cannot buy exceptional intellectual quotient, but the wisdom currency can. Let us together examine the story below:

And the king communed with them; AND AMONG THEM ALL WAS FOUND NONE LIKE DANIEL, HANANIAH, MISHAEL, AND AZARIAH: therefore stood they before the king. AND IN ALL MATTERS OF WISDOM and understanding, that the king inquired of them, HE FOUND THEM TEN TIMES BETTER THAN ALL the magicians and astrologers that were in all his realm. AND DANIEL CONTINUED EVEN UNTO THE FIRST YEAR OF KING CYRUS.

Dan 1:19-21

The story of a very outstanding and gifted American neurosurgeon named Ben Carson comes to mind. He was the first neurosurgeon to have successfully separated conjoined twins at the head. Numerous failed attempts were made by other surgeons to solve this particular problem. In such attempts, either one of the babies or both were lost in the surgery process. History was made by this surgeon in 1987, when he led a team of 70 doctors to successfully separate the Binder twins in 22 hours. Each twin survived and went on to lead individual lives[10]. Amazingly, Ben Carson was classified as a dummy while he was in fifth grade because he was doing poorly in class. But thank God he had a mother who, though was poor, knew it was possible for her son to become a distinguished man with a gifted mind. His mother though uneducated herself taught Ben how to tap into the wisdom currency. Under her parenting as a single mother, he blossomed into a great student who eventually went to medical school and became a world renowned neurosurgeon with specialization in separating conjoined twins[11]. He performed many other great feats as a neurosurgeon before retiring from the profession. By the wisdom currency, he developed new techniques for treating brain-stem tumors. As an approach for controlling seizures, he revived an unpopular technique known as hemispherectomy, which involved removing the diseased half of a patient's brain. Dr. Carson became the youngest chief of pediatric neurosurgery in the country at the age of 33. He received over 60 honorary doctorate degrees, several national merit citations, and has about a 100 neurosurgical publications to his name. He later moved on to politics and was the United State Secretary of Housing and Urban Development at the time of this writing[12]. This man has been known for his belief in Jesus Christ and is reputed for always making public, his stand for the gospel of the kingdom without compromise, just like Daniel. *I don't care to know your present status right now; I declare a divine impartation of wisdom on you in Jesus name! I see the manifestation of wisdom in your intellect, business, academics, profession, and on every member of your family in*

Jesus name! I see the wisdom currency distinguishing you and all that you do in Jesus name! By the time you are done reading this book, it will be evident that you have accessed an unusual dimension of wisdom.

2. *Wisdom currency can bring influence and promotion to its possessor.*

There are places where the naira, dollar, pounds and so on, cannot take you that wisdom would grant you access into. No matter how much wealth in earthly currency you have acquired, there are people you would never meet nor be able to reach out to without wisdom currency. However, even if you were a slave, a relative minor or you had no connections with the high and mighty in society, with wisdom currency, you can become a person of great influence. Daniel can tell you the story of his personal experience, about how wisdom granted him relevance in the reign of four different kingdoms. During the reign of king Nebuchadnezzar, the wisdom currency not only distinguished Daniel, but in addition, gave him so much influence with the King of Babylon, and as such received promotion from him. He then used his influence to request the promotion of his friends from the king. Let me remind you that this same Daniel was a Hebrew slave; yet, wisdom currency made the difference in his dealings with his colonial masters.

THEN THE KING NEBUCHADNEZZAR FELL UPON HIS FACE, AND WORSHIPPED DANIEL, AND COMMANDED THAT THEY SHOULD OFFER AN OBLATION AND SWEET ODOURS UNTO HIM. The king answered unto Daniel, and said, Of a truth it is, that your God is a God of gods, and a Lord of kings, and a revealer of secrets, seeing thou couldest reveal this secret. THEN THE KING MADE DANIEL A GREAT MAN, AND GAVE HIM MANY GREAT GIFTS, AND MADE HIM RULER OVER THE WHOLE PROVINCE OF BABYLON, AND CHIEF OF THE GOVERNORS OVER ALL THE WISE MEN OF BABYLON. THEN DANIEL REQUESTED OF THE KING, AND HE SET SHADRACH, MESHACH, AND ABED-NEGO, OVER THE AFFAIRS OF THE PROVINCE OF BABYLON: BUT DANIEL SAT IN THE GATE OF THE KING.

Dan 2:46-49

Joseph was not only a prisoner, but he was also a common slave who had no family ties in Egypt where he was imprisoned. Nonetheless, by reason of wisdom currency, he became so powerful and influential that he was granted authority over all of Egypt. The king made him next after him such that he was only greater than Joseph on the throne. The fact that he was an ex-convict slave was totally irrelevant. In our world today, some countries do not permit an ex-convict to even contest for an election talk more to become the Prime Minister. Most countries have constitutions that preclude slaves, non-indigenes or outcasts from handling positions of rulership, but Joseph's case was different. He was full of wisdom and that alone made the difference. Nobody could question his appointment because he bought them over by wisdom currency. *I pray for you today, that as you continue to transact with wisdom currency, you shall sit among kings in Jesus name!* The Bible says God is able to raise a beggar from the dunghill and set him up among princes (1 Sam 2:8). This shall be your testimony as you function in wisdom in Jesus name! Amen.

3. *Wisdom currency can procure tangible resources.*

If you need a house and you have the money in any earthly currency, there is a great likelihood that you will get it. In just the way paper money can be used to get some basic needs met, wisdom can also be engaged as a currency for procurement of things that paper money can or cannot buy even to greater measures. Wisdom is an intangible currency that can procure tangible resources like lands, houses, etc if accessed and converted. God, the creator King Himself, operated by wisdom when He set up the greatest piece of real estate ever known in the history of humanity called earth.

...That I may cause those that love me to inherit substance; and I will fill their treasures. THE LORD POSSESSED ME IN THE BEGINNING OF HIS WAY, BEFORE HIS WORKS OF OLD. I WAS SET UP FROM EVERLASTING, FROM THE BEGINNING, OR EVER THE EARTH WAS. WHEN THERE WERE NO DEPTHS, I WAS BROUGHT FORTH; WHEN THERE WERE NO FOUNTAINS ABOUNDING WITH WATER. BEFORE THE MOUNTAINS WERE SETTLED, BEFORE THE HILLS WAS I BROUGHT FORTH. WHILE AS YET HE HAD NOT MADE THE EARTH, NOR THE FIELDS, NOR THE HIGHEST PART OF THE DUST OF THE WORLD. WHEN HE PREPARED THE HEAVENS, I WAS THERE: when he set a compass upon the face of the depth: When he established the clouds above: when he strengthened the fountains of the deep.

The King of all creation sponsored the creation of the universe by the wisdom currency. If God could use this intangible currency to bring about the greatest piece of real estate, then we also who are His children can do same. No wonder the Bible says by wisdom, a house is built (Prov 24:3). That means you really do not need to worry about the amount of naira, dollar, pounds, euro, yen, etc that you have or can acquire now. What you need is wisdom currency, and when you have it and know how to convert it, you would be able to own much more than you can imagine on this earth and in any earthly currency. This is an awesome wonder!

4. ***Wisdom currency provides things that earthly currencies cannot buy:***

In our previous chapter, we saw some examples of wealthy, famous and influential people who despite these could not buy themselves happiness, fulfillment, health, joy and personal satisfaction. This is a bitter pill especially for those who have engaged in evil practices just to acquire wealth. Some have sold their souls to the devil in exchange for fame while others have mortgaged their destinies for glamour, only to discover that they are still lacking of things money and worldly fame cannot buy. This is where the superiority of kingdom currency becomes easier to see. The wisdom currency can be converted into tangible equivalents that riches cannot provide. Wisdom would provide you with a happy home where wealth can only build a big mansion. Wisdom will provide you with peace of mind where wealth can only provide you with more worries. Wisdom would teach you how to eat right despite the availability of abundance. Wisdom would grant you robust health and wellness that even the best hospital on earth cannot guarantee. The same is true for all the other kingdom currencies; they provide physical, spiritual and eternal benefits which are far beyond the reach of any earthly currency.

For such wisdom is far more valuable than precious jewels. Nothing else compares with it. WISDOM GIVES: a long, good life, RICHES, honor, pleasure, peace.

Proverbs 3:15-17 TLB

The above verse tells us that wisdom can bring different things into the life of a man who possesses wisdom. The good thing about this kingdom currency as earlier stated is that it does not only add riches to its possessor, it also adds things that earthly riches cannot provide in such a way that we can enjoy here on earth. All of the things listed in the scripture above are for kingdom citizens to enjoy here and now in this life, not in the sweet bye and bye. There are rich folks in the earthly kingdoms of this world today that lack long life. They also lack the God life which is the good life, and have lost every pint of honor because of the illicit nature of their riches. These folks lack peace because they have mortgaged their destinies for quick wealth. This observation is proof positive, that wisdom as a kingdom currency is a far better acquisition than earthly riches. This is so because the kingdom currency of wisdom can procure happiness, love, healthy relationships, peace, life, fulfillment, early satisfaction and all the finer things of life that even earthly money cannot buy.

5. ***Wisdom currency gives life which money cannot buy.***

The Bible says the fear of God is the beginning of wisdom. Anyone without the fear of God in him cannot have the life of God in him. He may amass wealth in earthly currency but he would still remain poor in the sight of Almighty God. To have the fear of God means to reverence God as the alpha and omega, the beginning and the end. The Bible tells us the story of a rich man who lived in magnificence. After the rich man died, he found himself in hell because when he was on earth he felt since he had money, he did not need God. That was the biggest mistake he ever made. When he saw that he was doomed in hell he cried out to Abraham begging for just a drop of water. A man who had so much money in earthly currency became miserable in hell. Money cannot buy eternal life but wisdom gives life. If you do not have this life, you can have it now. Refer to chapter one and say the prayer so that you would be granted access into the kingdom and its currencies.

For wisdom is a defence, and money is a defence: but the excellency of knowledge is, THAT WISDOM GIVETH LIFE TO THEM THAT HAVE IT.

Eccl 7:12

Wisdom is a more dependable defense over money and based on that it is a greater asset to be desired. Wisdom must be given precedence over money in the minds of every kingdom citizen in terms of importance. When this takes place you would surely enjoy the benefits of this kingdom currency.

6. *With the wisdom currency you big projects can be facilitated without having problems with contractors.*

Solomon wanted to build a befitting edifice for temple worship and he used wisdom currency to sort out everything pertaining to payments and good customer relations. Some people employ the services of a contractor and end up with an unnecessary quarrel and misunderstanding due to their lack of wisdom and unfaithfulness. Of course there are cases where you may be a victim of poor services from contractors but with wisdom, you can make up for all that. Here's what the Bible says about Solomon's dealings with a building contractor known as King Hiram:

So Hiram sent word to Solomon: "I have received the message you sent me and will do all you want in providing the cedar and pine logs. My men will haul them down from Lebanon to the sea, and I will float them in rafts by sea to the place you specify. There I will separate them and you can take them away. AND YOU ARE TO GRANT MY WISH BY PROVIDING FOOD FOR MY ROYAL HOUSEHOLD." IN THIS WAY HIRAM KEPT SOLOMON SUPPLIED WITH ALL THE CEDAR AND PINE LOGS HE WANTED, AND SOLOMON GAVE HIRAM TWENTY THOUSAND CORS OF WHEAT AS FOOD FOR HIS HOUSEHOLD, in addition to twenty thousand baths of pressed olive oil. Solomon continued to do this for Hiram year after year. THE LORD GAVE SOLOMON WISDOM, JUST AS HE HAD PROMISED

HIM. THERE WERE PEACEFUL RELATIONS BETWEEN HIRAM AND SOLOMON, AND THE TWO OF THEM MADE A TREATY.

1 Kings 5:6-12 NIV

When you operate with wisdom, you can do business wisely and end up every contract you do with peaceful relations. Those who end business transactions in unnecessary quarrels, fights and arguments are not operating the wisdom currency. Wisdom would enable you pay for the services of everyone who works for you no matter the size of the project. Even when there is a breach of contract, wisdom would enable you know when to walk away peacefully before any unhealthy event comes up.

7. *Wisdom currency can fetch you big contracts without lobbying or even bidding.*

The story of a certain Mr. Hiram, the son of a widow comes to mind. The wisest king from a foreign country wanted to set up several massive structures that required exceptional expertise. Despite the vastness of the king's empire, the king did not give this contract to anyone out of the thousands of craftsmen in his empire. Rather, the king went as far as another city in a different empire to fetch this man because he was known to be full of wisdom and craftsmanship. This man got a contract he never bidded for. He just got a message that a king in another nation needs his services, and that was how his name became recorded in the greatest books of all time. The king who gave him the contract was King Solomon (1 Kings 7:13-45 NIV).

AND KING SOLOMON SENT AND FETCHED HIRAM OUT OF TYRE. He was a widow's son of the tribe of Naphtali, and his father was a man of Tyre, a worker in brass: AND HE WAS FILLED WITH WISDOM, AND UNDERSTANDING, AND CUNNING TO WORK ALL WORKS IN BRASS. AND HE CAME TO KING SOLOMON, AND WROUGHT ALL HIS WORK.

1 Kings 7:13-14

Wisdom always distinguishes its possessors. When you function with the wisdom of God in anything you do, people would look for you for the solutions which you are known for providing. Hiram was on his own in another nation when the wisdom currency brought for him a heavy contract job. He did not need any connection to get the contract from the king; rather the wisdom currency connected him despite the distance.

8. *Wisdom currency can be used to sponsor building projects.*

If God the Creator King sponsored the greatest construction project in all of history with the wisdom currency, it means we who are His children can also take advantage of the wisdom currency in performing similar requirements which we normally do with paper monies. The scripture makes us understand that wisdom causes the children of the Kingdom to inherit substance. It says it will fill their treasures, that is to say store houses, banks, treasuries, repositories (Prov 8:21). That same passage goes further to speak about how God possessed wisdom before carrying out His works of Creation. The verse says, "...*the Lord POSSESSED me in the beginning of His way...*" You see how we can achieve great things on earth if we possess wisdom as a currency. We can build houses and get other things which we need by the wisdom currency even when it looks like our physical monetary capacity is limited.

THROUGH WISDOM IS A HOUSE BUILT;

Prov 24:3 NIV

This is because the wisdom currency can procure what we need with or without the paper money. Sometimes, wisdom currency may produce paper monies for us to get those things, but at other times it may just provide the actual thing we needed money for. This is a great spiritual reality that can cause us to get all the provisions God has for us here on earth. If we begin to apply it, we can truly enjoy kingdom currency.

9. *Wisdom currency begets fame, though fame does not beget wisdom.*

Another word for fame is reputation, name and renown. When a man is known for wisdom, he would be renowned for mighty deeds, and this would attract recognition and attention from society. Fame in itself, is not a bad thing; it can be an asset if used properly and correctly. However, it can be corrupted and it can also corrupt individuals, especially those who lack character and integrity. What you do with fame when it comes matters a lot. When fame comes, it must be used as a medium to preach the message of the kingdom and to draw men unto Jesus Christ. Fame does not make anyone wise, but wisdom can make you famous and when this happens men will want to hear you. People would want to interview you to ask about your secret, and that would be a great opportunity to declare the gospel of Christ and the kingdom. Wisdom can cause your name to be heard in nations where you have not even been to physically. It can bring you before great men like it did for Daniel, Joseph and several characters in both Bible days and contemporary times.

WHEN THE QUEEN OF SHEBA HEARD OF SOLOMON'S FAME, WHICH BROUGHT HONOR TO THE NAME OF THE LORD, SHE CAME TO TEST HIM WITH HARD QUESTIONS. She arrived in Jerusalem with a large group of attendants and a great caravan of camels loaded with spices, large quantities of gold, and precious jewels. When she met with Solomon, she talked with him about everything she had on her mind. Solomon had answers for all her questions; nothing was too hard for the king to explain to her. When the queen of Sheba realized how very wise Solomon was, and when she saw the palace he had built, she was overwhelmed. She was also amazed at the food on his tables, the organization of his officials and their splendid clothing, the cup-bearers, and the burnt offerings Solomon made at the Temple of the Lord. SHE EXCLAIMED TO THE KING, "EVERYTHING I HEARD IN MY COUNTRY ABOUT YOUR

ACHIEVEMENTS AND WISDOM IS TRUE! I didn't believe what was said until I arrived here and saw it with my own eyes. In fact, I had not heard the half of it! YOUR WISDOM AND PROSPERITY ARE FAR BEYOND WHAT I WAS TOLD. How happy your people must be! What a privilege for your officials to stand here day after day, listening to your wisdom! Praise the Lord your God, who delights in you and has placed you on the throne of Israel. Because of the Lord's eternal love for Israel, he has made you king so you can rule with justice and righteousness." THEN SHE GAVE THE KING A GIFT OF 9,000 POUNDS OF GOLD, GREAT QUANTITIES OF SPICES, AND PRECIOUS JEWELS. Never again were so many spices brought in as those the queen of Sheba gave to King Solomon.

1 Kings 10:1-10

Fame can help you spread the gospel of the kingdom faster. Solomon's fame brought the queen of Sheba all the way from the east to his palace because she wanted to see for herself and hear for herself. On this occasion, Solomon used his influence and fame correctly. The wisdom of Solomon carried so much power and anointing that the Queen fainted just by the words that came out of Solomon's mouth. The

King James Version says there was no more spirit in her after she encountered Solomon (1 Kings 10:5). She later testified that what she heard was nothing compared to what she had come to witness for herself. If Solomon was not famous, he would never have had the opportunity to minister wisdom to the Queen of Sheba. So fame is among the ancillary benefits that go with the wisdom currency.

HE WAS WISER THAN ANY OTHER MAN, including Ethan the Ezrahite — wiser than Heman, Calcol and Darda, the sons of Mahol. AND HIS FAME SPREAD TO ALL THE SURROUNDING NATIONS.

1 Kings 4:31 NIV

Jesus the King, when He walked the earth grew in wisdom. Because Jesus had increased in wisdom, when He was to begin ministry, He did not need publicity to announce His ministry because His fame spread abroad. Jesus was famous for many things and wisdom is one of them. The more wisdom currency you possess, the more famous you can become, and that fame would be used to spread the kingdom even faster.

CHAPTER FIVE

HOW TO TURN WISDOM CURRENCY INTO MONEY

1. Be a problem solver, think of genuine solutions to people's problems.

One way to convert the kingdom currency of wisdom is to always think of solutions. Never be problem conscious but solution driven. Whenever you preoccupy yourself with problems in such a way that you begin to complain, you shut down your creative capacity. Joseph got himself a wonderful promotion, a "wife gift", the king's ring which symbolizes authority, fine clothes, the king's second chariot, and the king's honor. How did he come about these bounties? He helped the king solve his problems.

LET PHARAOH DO THIS, AND LET HIM APPOINT OFFICERS OVER THE LAND, AND TAKE UP THE FIFTH PART OF THE LAND OF EGYPT IN THE SEVEN PLENTEOUS YEARS. AND LET THEM GATHER ALL THE FOOD OF THOSE GOOD YEARS THAT COME, AND LAY UP CORN UNDER THE HAND OF PHARAOH, AND LET THEM KEEP FOOD IN THE CITIES. AND THAT FOOD SHALL BE FOR STORE TO THE LAND AGAINST THE SEVEN YEARS OF FAMINE, WHICH SHALL BE IN THE LAND OF EGYPT; THAT THE LAND PERISH NOT THROUGH THE FAMINE. And the thing was good in the eyes of Pharaoh, and in the eyes of all his servants. And Pharaoh said unto his servants, Can we find such a one as this is, a man in whom the Spirit of God is? AND PHARAOH SAID UNTO JOSEPH, FORASMUCH AS GOD HATH SHEWED THEE ALL

THIS, THERE IS NONE SO DISCREET AND WISE AS THOU ART: THOU SHALT BE OVER MY HOUSE, AND ACCORDING UNTO THY WORD SHALL ALL MY PEOPLE BE RULED: ONLY IN THE THRONE WILL I BE GREATER THAN THOU. AND PHARAOH SAID UNTO JOSEPH, SEE, I HAVE SET THEE OVER ALL THE LAND OF EGYPT. AND PHARAOH TOOK OFF HIS RING FROM HIS HAND, AND PUT IT UPON JOSEPH'S HAND, AND ARRAYED HIM IN VESTURES OF FINE LINEN, AND PUT A GOLD CHAIN ABOUT HIS NECK; AND HE MADE HIM TO RIDE IN THE SECOND CHARIOT WHICH HE HAD; AND THEY CRIED BEFORE HIM, BOW THE KNEE: AND HE MADE HIM RULER OVER ALL THE LAND OF EGYPT. AND PHARAOH SAID UNTO JOSEPH, I AM PHARAOH, AND WITHOUT THEE SHALL NO MAN LIFT UP HIS HAND OR FOOT IN ALL THE LAND OF EGYPT. AND PHARAOH CALLED JOSEPH'S NAME ZAPHNATH-PAANEAH; AND HE GAVE HIM TO WIFE ASENATH THE DAUGHTER OF POTI-PHERAH PRIEST OF ON. And Joseph went out over all the land of Egypt.

Gen 41:34-46 KJV

2. Seek to add value to others.

Joseph was always eager to leave people with a smile on their faces. He had an amazing personality, his smile was his logo. He was in the business of making dejected and sad people happy. How you leave others feeling after an encounter with you becomes your trademark. He was very sensitive to his environment and swift to offer his gifts when the need presented itself. This attitude made him get a bigger platform to display his wisdom.

WHEN JOSEPH CAME TO THEM THE NEXT MORNING, HE SAW THAT THEY WERE DEJECTED. SO HE ASKED Pharaoh's officials who were in custody with him in his master's house, "WHY ARE YOUR FACES SO SAD TODAY?" "We both had dreams," they answered, "but there is no one to interpret them." Then Joseph said to them, "Do not interpretations belong to God? Tell me your dreams."

Gen 40:6-8 NIV

After Joseph interpreted the dreams for the two of them, even though they forgot him immediately, it was this singular experience that drew the cup bearers attention back to Joseph and granted him the greatest opportunity to serve his gifts on a large scale. The wisest king in the Old Testament, was recorded to be the richest king of all time before the King of kings, Jesus came on the scene. This was a function of the wisdom the man possessed and was able to harness and convert. Solomon's wealth did not just come by magic, wisdom produced them.

3. Discover what you can offer as a good or service and market it creatively.

There are many talented and gifted people who have taken their gifts into the graveyard. They were known for their talent only by their family and friends and they did not do more than use their gifting in their comfort zone. They did not know how to market their gifting to the right target market. They were afraid to attach monetary value to what they have to offer in meeting a need in the society.

SO KING SOLOMON EXCEEDED ALL THE KINGS OF THE EARTH FOR RICHES AND FOR WISDOM. AND ALL THE EARTH SOUGHT TO SOLOMON, TO HEAR HIS WISDOM, WHICH GOD HAD PUT IN HIS HEART. AND THEY BROUGHT EVERY MAN HIS PRESENT, vessels of silver, and vessels of gold, and garments, and armour, and spices, horses, and mules, A RATE YEAR BY YEAR.

1 Kings 10:23-25

Solomon was full of wisdom and he knew he could use it to add value to people all over the world. He began to organize seminars and people all over the world came to listen to his wisdom. The Bible records that everyone who attended Solomon's seminars came with his present. They were made to give a certain rate yearly as appreciation for the values that were deposited in them by the wisdom Solomon had. Solomon discovered his strength and offered it in service to people who in turn were more than willing to pay for his services. Think of a service you can offer to people which you are passionate about and which you would not mind doing for free. Think of a creative way you can organize that talent or gift in a manner that people would not mind to pay something just to receive that service. That was what Solomon did and it contributed greatly to his wealth. Solomon was a writer and composer of songs and that is what produced the song book titled Songs of Solomon. He wrote many books in order to communicate his wisdom even when he is no more on earth. There is a saying that everyone on earth has a book inside of him, or a song or art inside of him. Do you have an idea, story or a message that you want to share with the whole world? Then put it down in form of articles, audio-visual recordings, books and publications. These materials will still be speaking to many generations after you are gone from this earth. And if you allow God guide you in doing it, that simple art would bring you before kings and queens just like Solomon.

4. Be a researcher in areas where solutions have not been discovered.

Wisdom is known as the insight into the true nature of things. There are many things that are yet to be searched out of the wells of wisdom. There are many insights people have not even conceive to be possible. If you know you have the wisdom currency, you can embark on a research journey to discover some of these insights. You can discover the antidote for cancer. You can research on how to make something or do something in a more efficient manner. You can identify something totally unknown to humanity by the wisdom currency and that would bring you so many opportunities. Solomon, the wisest king of old, was known for his many research and discoveries. His wisdom was always put to work to produce tangible results.

AND SOLOMON'S WISDOM EXCELLED THE WISDOM OF ALL THE CHILDREN OF THE EAST COUNTRY, AND ALL THE WISDOM OF EGYPT. For he was wiser than all men; than Ethan the Ezrahite, and Heman, and Chalcol, and Darda, the sons of Mahol: and his fame was in all nations round about. AND HE SPAKE THREE THOUSAND PROVERBS: AND HIS SONGS WERE A THOUSAND AND FIVE. AND HE SPAKE OF TREES, FROM THE

CEDAR TREE THAT IS IN LEBANON EVEN UNTO THE HYSSOP THAT SPRINGETH OUT OF THE WALL: HE SPAKE ALSO OF BEASTS, AND OF FOWL, AND OF CREEPING THINGS, AND OF FISHES. And there came of all people to hear the wisdom of Solomon, from all kings of the earth, which had heard of his wisdom.

1 Kings 4:30-34

Solomon's research archive was so full that he spoke of 3000 proverbs. A proverb is an expression of basic truth which has been discovered and can be applied to practical life situations. Solomon sang 1005 songs and in today's world that can produce 150 albums of 10 tracks each. Songs are messages clothed in melodies and with songs you can communicate a discovery, provoke deep imagination and inspire possibilities. He researched on different trees, including the cedar trees in Lebanon. Solomon was such a gifted researcher that even the hyssop that grew on the walls in the houses of Jerusalem caught his attention and he began researching on them. He studied even the beasts of the field in their diversities, the creeping creatures in their uniqueness and even fishes. After making these researches, he began to teach and speak about these ideas and discoveries to people in his seminars. No wonder he said a wise man shall hear and increase in learning. Now you have heard of the exploits which Solomon did. You may not need to study thousands of subjects to convert wisdom into tangible wealth. But you would need to research on anything that catches your attention and get insight into the true nature of that thing. When you do this, get that insight published, tell the world about it, and they would seek to hear you speak and would not mind exchanging their monies for that.

5. Do everything within your power to make people who do business with you happy with your services.

Many people do not know the value of good customer and business relations. They treat their customers like a "nobody" especially when it seems they have grown and have become popular. This is a sure ticket to a gradual loss of future business growth. If you want to sustain growth and prosperity in any endeavor whether as a contractor, business man, captain of industry, or president, you must make it a duty to leave your customers happy after every transaction. If you are a leader, you must give the people you are privileged to lead the best service. This is not to say you would compromise core values in a bid to please people. But make a conscious effort to put a smile on the face of those you are called to serve with your goods and services by doing what is right.

THERE WERE PEACEFUL RELATIONS BETWEEN HIRAM AND SOLOMON, AND THE TWO OF THEM MADE A TREATY.

1 **Kings 5: 12**

6. Always engage in wise planning.

For every idea, innovation or vision, there is a provision. The provision normally comes along with the vision. It is left for the conceiver of the idea to figure out how to get the provision to drive his business idea. This is where wise planning becomes very essential. If you have an idea, without the capital to fund it, it means you lack wise planning. This is because every vision (idea) carries with it a provision to implement and sustain it.

Any enterprise is built by wise planning, becomes strong through common sense, and profits wonderfully by keeping abreast of the facts.

Prov 24:3-4 TLB

The King James Version of Proverbs 24:3 says "...through wisdom a house is built". The Living Bible puts it this way "...any enterprise (business) is built by wise planning". Only through wise planning can you discern the channel through which the required resources will show up. The kingdom currency of wisdom is all you need to start a family, build a home and build a billion dollar enterprise (Prov 24:3 AMP) not your local bank, rich uncle, or highly connected friend or brother. The truth is if you convert your ideas into workable plans, probably a viable business plan or a workable family plan to fend for your potential wife or future family, the resources will begin to gravitate towards you from all the corners of the earth. This is one among many other ways to convert the kingdom currency of wisdom into the money you require to fund that idea of yours. It is wise planning, not illusions of grandeur. Receive the spirit of wisdom now and begin to do exploits, let your mind be inundated with the insight for foresight, as you ponder on this article in Jesus name!

7. Do not despise your little beginning.

It is foolish to despise little beginnings and not see the potential future of a small seed. Every wise farmer knows the value of little seeds in cultivating a great tree, and furthermore a forest. A wise man, Dr. Myles Munroe said, in every seed, there is a forest. How true! Some ladies despise great suitors because they do not have a mansion and a nice car, forgetting that this young man has an established vision that will produce abundance of those things in future. Anything that appears big will experience big challenges, which can only be handled by one who has been trained overtime through constant practice of smaller things which are similar and related to the big things.

Who despises the day of small things...

Zech 4:10 NIV

If you want to do business and succeed, start relatively small; do not wait until everything is perfect. Look beyond the immediate, and plan for the best in the near future. A young athlete who dreams to be a successful competitor in the Olympic Games event of 10,000m marathon does not start out with 10,000m. He starts from a shorter distance like 1,000m and then he progresses, improves and increases his capacity until he reaches that of a 10,000m marathon racer. No boxer, no matter the dreams for greatness he has, starts doing pushups the first day he joined the boxing academy as a teenager or youth. He starts small, with 5 pushups then moves to 10, then 15, then 20... and so on until his muscles develop capacity for 100 even to and beyond 500 pushups.

Anyone who despises little beginnings will not be able to convert the wisdom currency.

8. Do not labor foolishly.

Many people think the more they grind on the mill, and engage in hard labor, the wealthier they will become. They cannot be further from the truth. If wealth were to be by hard labor, then the truck pushers and bricklayers would be the wealthiest men in the world. But this is not the case, because only wise labor produces material results. The Bible teaches this principle in the scripture below:

Do not wear yourself out to get rich; have the wisdom to show restraint.

Prov 23:4 NIV

The real work is in the mind's ability to identify problems and think of a dynamic way to proffer solutions to such problems. The moment this happens, you would discover that work becomes purposeful and goal oriented, plus it will be sponsored by wisdom. On the other hand, when money is the goal in your attitude towards work, you may never be able to enjoy the money. There is a better way you can achieve greater results with less efforts. This was what led to the greatest inventions of all time, the wisdom to find less cumbersome ways for communication, transportation, recreation, etc. The moment you engage the wisdom currency, such ideas will begin to crystallize in your mind, and as you translate those divine insight into reality, there is no telling how much wealth will gravitate towards you.

9. Involve the best quality resources, manpower and expertise in developing your insights or ideas into reality.

Never substitute quality for cheap labor because every idea will be branded according to the quality of minds that work on its development. Donald Trump before he became President of the United States was known for being a wealthy real estate billionaire developer. His company, the Trump Organization is known for erecting the best quality structures in the best locations around the world. He emerged among the richest men in the world because of his value for taste, and quality service which in the long haul, distinguished him as the most excellent in the field of real estate. He is reputed for giving superior quality, detailing and perfection in all his structures, employing the best architects in the world on each project. He loves to erect quality structures no matter what it takes and when he completes such project, people do not mind paying double or triple what other structures are worth, just to get the quality which Trump's brand offers. This is wisdom and Solomon displayed it when he took on the project of building the temple. He contracted the best workmen and got the best services, and this was a function of the wisdom currency.

And, behold, I PURPOSE TO BUILD AN HOUSE UNTO THE NAME OF THE LORD MY GOD, as the Lord spake unto David my father, saying, Thy son, whom I will set upon thy throne in thy room, he shall build an house unto my name. NOW THEREFORE COMMAND THOU THAT THEY HEW ME CEDAR TREES OUT OF LEBANON; AND MY SERVANTS SHALL BE WITH THY SERVANTS: AND UNTO THEE WILL I GIVE HIRE FOR THY SERVANTS ACCORDING TO ALL THAT THOU SHALT APPOINT: FOR THOU KNOWEST THAT THERE IS NOT AMONG US ANY THAT CAN SKILL TO HEW TIMBER LIKE UNTO THE SIDONIANS. And it came to pass, when Hiram heard the words of Solomon, that he rejoiced greatly, and said, Blessed be the Lord this day, which hath given unto David a WISE son over this great people.

Solomon was called wise because he decided to go all the way to King Hiram, king of Tyre to get the best expertise, and his wisdom paid off as the temple which was built by him came out so excellently. In fact, the Bible says the house was built without the use of hammer, axe or any tool of iron (1 Kings 6:7). This was a high level civil engineering technique which only top class veterans in construction can perform.

10. Be an expert in your field no matter what field it is.

Many nations, international organizations and corporations are looking for extraordinary people to take on tasks that are heavily wisdom intensive. They would go any length to get the best hands on a job, and they have their eyes looking everywhere for such expertise. If you can distinguish yourself in any field where you know you have a competitive advantage by using the wisdom currency, you are the next in line for a multi-billion dollar deal. The man Hiram was not an influential man in Jerusalem. His mother was from a tribe in Israel which can be seen as a minority and his father was from Tyre. He was more like a half-caste to the Israelites. Regardless of this, Solomon had no choice but to give that man the job even without him applying for it. The Bible recorded that they went to fetch him because, he by wisdom currency had established himself as an expert in his field.

And king Solomon sent and fetched Hiram out of Tyre. He was a widow's son of the tribe of Naphtali, and his father was a man of Tyre, a worker in brass: and he was filled with wisdom, and understanding, and cunning to work all works in brass. And he came to king Solomon, and wrought all his work.

1 Kings 7:13-14

CHARGE

Never make getting money a priority in your life as a kingdom citizen because money is not the real issue. You can have a billion dollar today and still not be happy. A wealthy man today can lose all his wealth in a second and become miserable in the twinkle of an eye. But if you possess wisdom currency, you will know how to generate a billion dollar from scratch or sustain the growth of your billion dollar wealth at any level. If you want happiness in your life and relationships, never make money a priority in choosing a friend or a life partner. For the Bible says, "...The man who knows right from wrong, has good judgment and common sense is happier than the man who is immensely rich!" (Prov 3:13-15 TLB). Make wisdom your priority, after all, money pursues after wisdom. Always be conscious of the fact that you are a kingdom specie and you seek first the kingdom of God in all you do as a kingdom citizen (Matt 6:33). You operate kingdom currency, which out values any currency you can think of in this world. Beloved, get wisdom because it has many more advantages than what has been listed in this chapter. It is your key to unending prosperity and security. It's in your Kingdom Central Bank (Christ), waiting for you to make withdrawals, through the Central Bank Governor (the Holy Spirit). God wants you to be rich as a kingdom citizen, but He wants you to get wisdom first (Prov 4:7). For then you can become rich in all things, including things earthly currencies cannot buy. Be blessed as you ponder on these kingdom verities in Jesus name!

CONFESSION

I have the wisdom of God in me. I am loaded with the wisdom currency of the kingdom of God. Nothing takes me unawares and I am not a victim of fraud and deception. I walk in the wisdom of God for my health, academics, finances, family and everywhere I go. I have access to the wisdom bank of God and I know what to do to convert this heavenly currency of mine into tangible products. I am wise and I do not walk in confusion. The fame of my wisdom spreads across all nations of the earth. I have more opportunities and platforms to display the wisdom of God upon my life. I am a problem solver, a solution provider. I was born as an answer to the cry of billions of people. Kings and queens, men in high places are looking for me to offer them of my wisdom currency. They locate me speedily from all corners of the earth. I am wise and prosperous. I know how to convert this heavenly currency into tangible wealth and I am putting it to practice in Jesus name! Amen.

REFERENCES

1. 10 unbelievable inheritance stories, https://www.oddee.com/item_96948.aspx, accessed 19/06/2017.

2. Josie Siler, "Your inheritance is waiting", October 23, 2012, https://www.oddee.com/item_96948.aspx, accessed 19/6/2017.

3. Central Bank - Wikipedia, the free encyclopedia, https://en.wikipedia.org/wiki/Central_bank, accessed 5/7/2017.

Other Books by the author are:

- ➢ **How To Turn Your Knowledge To Money**
- ➢ **How To Make Money From What You Understand**
- ➢ **Unlocking Your Kingdom Creativity**
- ➢ **How To Make Millions As an AuthorPreneur**
- ➢ **How To Maximize Kingdom Currency**
- ➢ **Kingdom Currency for Students, Graduates and Business Men**
- ➢ **Kingdom Verities Volume One**
- ➢ **How To Enjoy Kingdom Currency**

Each of these titles can be ordered in bulk quantities from Forcible Publications when contacted via details provided in the copyright page.

To contact us for feedback, testimonies, and partnerships or to schedule the author for presentations, keynotes and other matters of discussion, please send a mail to:

forciblepublications@gmail.com

Or call (+234) 8173862018

Social media handle: iredafeowolabi

Website: iredafeowolabi.net

ABOUT THE AUTHOR

Iredafenevesho Owolabi is a seasoned teacher and preacher of the message of the Kingdom of God. He is happily married to Pharm. Dr. Precious Owolabi, the love of his life and together they are affecting lives for the Kingdom. He holds a BEng Chemical Engineering, University of Benin and He is a Software Developer. The literal meaning of his first name is "the kingdom of God has come into my house". That is why he is popularly called "the Kingdom Man".

He facilitates seminars, trainings, workshops and conferences for schools, banks, businesses, churches and organizations around the world.

He runs an online coaching program tagged Creativity Accelertor with the goal of helping individuals and organisations move from idea to profitable creations. People who desire to make an impact in the world are being guided to reach their highest potentials through this program.

Some of his talks and seminars include:

Millions from Book Idea: Discover how to grow and generate a six to seven figure enterprise from a book idea. Learn the hacks of the book development process, book publishing process, book sales process and and the book marketing process.

Leadership Mastery: How to bring out the leader in you, your staffs or any group of individuals. How to be a more effective leader in every area of business and life. Discover how the top leaders think and act in every area of personal and business life. Identify your personal and corporate value, commit to your inner self and position yourself for leadership success.

Becoming a Kingdom Businessman: Discover the secrets of profound kingdom businessmen who lived in modern contemporary times with extraordinary results. Discover kingdom keys to becoming God's kind of business professional who has superior skills, strategy and solutions for real problems.

Corporate Creativity and Intrapreneurship: How to create, invent and proffer solutions for the benefit of mankind in a profitable manner. How to release your creative potential and that of those who work with you and for you.

Peak Performance Creativity, Productivity and Profitability: How to multiply your results and scale up profits through innovation and 21st century thinking. How to create value in which customers would find continuous satisfation.

ONLINE COURSES AND PROGRAMS BY IREDAFENEVESHO OWOLABI INCLUDES:

Currency Converter: Helps you understand intangible currencies and convert them to any physical currency or material wealth that you can enjoy here and now. Helps you identify your true wealth and shows you how to tap into it.

Also helps you build genuine wealth from the scratch. It reveals to you the secret of money and shows you principles and strategies that would help you generate large sums of it.

Creativity Accelerator: Refines your critical thinking and complex problem solving skills in a way that positions you for greater promotion and opportunities. Helps you to initiate positive change in your career and business. Shows you how to stay relevant and gain prominence in your industry as the Fourth Industrial Revolution approaches.

WANT TO BOOK IREDAFENEVESHO?

Iredafenevesho Owolabi would carefully customize his talk for you and your audience. Call today for full information on booking Iredafenevesho Owolabi to speak at your next meeting or conference. Visit www.iredafeowolabi.net, phone (+234) 8187960599 or send a mail to info@iredafeowolabi.net or iredafeowolabi@gmail.com.

Social Media Handles

Instagram: @iredafeowolabi

Facebook: @iredafeowolabi

Linkedin: @iredafeowolabi

Twitter: @iredafeowolabi